INSIDE THE SYNAGOGUE

REVISED EDITION

*by Joan G. Sugarman
and Grace R. Freeman*

•

*photography by Ronald Mass
and others*

UNION OF AMERICAN HEBREW CONGREGATIONS

New York

THIS BOOK
IS
DEDICATED
TO THE
CHILDREN
WE HAVE TAUGHT
AND
FROM WHOM WE
HAVE LEARNED SO MUCH

—JOAN G. SUGARMAN
—GRACE R. FREEMAN

Revised edition © Copyright 1984 by
THE UNION OF AMERICAN HEBREW CONGREGATIONS

Manufactured in the United States of America

9 8 7 6 5 4 3 2 1

Introduction

For more than two decades, for tens of thousands of Jewish children, *Inside the Synagogue* has served as a first introduction to the temple, its symbols, rituals, and leaders. In truth, and deservedly so, it has become a classic in Jewish education, for both the Jewish school and the Jewish home.

This newly revised edition, with photographs by Rabbi Ronald Mass, ensures that the genius of Joan G. Sugarman and Grace R. Freeman will touch a whole new generation of parents and children. For this, we at the UAHC are grateful. Special thanks are due to Stuart Benick, UAHC Director of Publications, Steven Schnur, Josette Knight, and all those readers who, over the years, have offered suggestions designed to enhance and strengthen the text.

Our joy is diminished by the loss of Grace Freeman, a gifted teacher, a brilliant writer, and a deeply committed Jew. We dedicate this newly revised edition to her memory, in the words of her rabbi, Rabbi Joseph P. Weinberg:

> "Our tradition teaches us 'If you have learned much Torah, do not hold fast to it for yourself, but teach it to others, for thereto were you created.' This was the motto by which Grace Freeman lived her life."

May her memory and the fruits of her work be a blessing to this and future generations.

DANIEL B. SYME
Director of Education

Chapter One

The Synagogue Today

Wherever Jews go, we build a House of God. Sometimes this building is called a synagogue. Sometimes it is called a temple.

Some synagogues and temples are very old; others are new. Some are built of wood; others, of brick or stone. But old or new, brick, stone, or wood, a synagogue is a place where Jews go:

> to pray to God,
> to learn about our religion,
> to meet other Jews.

In this book, we are going to visit a House of God. We will find out how Jews pray to God, how we learn about our religion, and how we work to help each other. But first we will learn how the earliest synagogues and temples were created.

Chapter Two

How Synagogues Began

The very first Jewish temple was a tent in the desert, called the Tabernacle. After King David decided that Jerusalem would become the chief city for the children of Israel, his son, King Solomon, built a great Temple there. The room with the Holy Ark was called the Holy of Holies. It was so holy only the high priest entered it—and only once a year, on Yom Kippur, our most solemn holy day. The ancient Israelites believed that God's Spirit lived in the Temple in Jerusalem. So they came there to worship and offer sacrifices to God.

After many years, very wise Jews sensed that God was not only in the Temple of Jerusalem, but that God was everywhere. They said to the people: "God is everywhere. You may worship God any-where. You can study God's Torah everywhere." So the people began to meet in houses. They called them synagogues, after the Greek word for "meeting place." And from that time down to this day, Jews build synagogues or temples wherever they live.

Chapter Three

The Oldest Temples in the United States

The first Jewish settlers, a group of twenty-three men and women, came to the United States in 1654. When they landed in New York City, they found no synagogue because no Jews had ever lived there before. So their first services were held in their homes.

Later, they built a synagogue on Mill Street in New York City. It was the first synagogue in the United States. That small, wooden building is gone now.

As more and more Jews came to the United States, they settled in other cities. Groups of families came together and built more synagogues. Jewish communities built synagogues in cities like Savannah, Georgia; Philadelphia, Pennsylvania; Charleston, South Carolina; Richmond, Virginia; and Newport, Rhode Island.

These early synagogues were important. They brought the Jews together, helped newcomers, and showed Jews in foreign lands that America was a land of religious freedom. When Jews came to America from Europe, South America, and Asia, they first went to the synagogue. There they were welcomed, given a place to stay, and made to feel that they belonged to a family of Jews.

THE SYNAGOGUE OF CHARLESTON, S.C.

Erected 1795 Destroyed by Fire 27th Apl 1838.

This print is Dedicated with Great respect to Judah A. Motta Esqr.

by his very obedient and obliged Friend.

Solomon N Carvalho

Chapter Four

The Touro Synagogue

In the city of Newport, Rhode Island, is the oldest synagogue building still standing in the United States.

The synagogue is called the Touro Synagogue, in honor of its first rabbi, Isaac Touro.

The Touro Synagogue opened on the second day of December in 1763. An English architect, named Peter Harrison, planned the building. It has 186,715 bricks in it—all brought over from England. No nails were used in building it—only wooden pegs.

Inside, at the center, is a raised platform called the bimah. The man reading the Torah stood on the bimah. Around the bimah, in a square, are pews. Men sat downstairs. Women sat upstairs on a balcony with a rail around it.

The Touro Synagogue has a very important letter. It was written by President George Washington to an officer of the synagogue. It says that all Americans are free to worship God as they wish.

In 1946, the United States government put up a plaque saying that the building is a national shrine—important to all Americans.

NATIONAL HISTORIC SITE
TOURO SYNAGOGUE
OF
JESHUAT ISRAEL CONGREGATION
FOUNDED 1658

THIS OLDEST SYNAGOGUE BUILDING IN THE
UNITED STATES WAS DESIGNED BY PETER
HARRISON. GROUND WAS BROKEN AUGUST 1,
1759. IT WAS DEDICATED ON DECEMBER 2, 1763.
HERE 1781-84 THE RHODE ISLAND GENERAL
ASSEMBLY MET, AND DURING WASHINGTON'S
VISIT TO NEWPORT IN 1781 A TOWN
MEETING WAS HELD HERE. THE STATE SUPREME
COURT HELD SESSIONS HERE AT THAT PERIOD.
THE BUILDING WAS REOPENED FOR RELIGIOUS
SERVICES ON AUGUST 2, 1850. IN 1790 GEORGE
WASHINGTON WROTE TO THIS CONGREGATION
THAT..."HAPPILY THE GOVERNMENT OF THE
UNITED STATES....GIVES TO BIGOTRY NO
SANCTION, TO PERSECUTION NO ASSISTANCE."

NATIONAL
PARK SERVICE

UNITED STATES
DEPARTMENT OF THE INTERIOR

Chapter Five

Starting a Temple

Every year many Jewish families move to towns—and even countries—where there are no synagogues. But they want to share with other Jews their prayers, their learning, and their celebrations. So they meet together with Jewish families living nearby and decide to form a congregation—one big family—so that they can all worship and study together.

At first they worship in a house, an empty store, or a hall. There they begin a religious school for their children and plan ways to build a synagogue and a school. Together, little by little, they save their money and together they dream of building a permanent house for prayer and study.

Months pass, sometimes years. The congregation grows larger. Boys and girls celebrate Bar and Bat Mitzvah and Confirmation. And finally the congregation saves enough money to hire an architect to plan their synagogue building. Then they pay for bricks and marble and concrete. And one glorious day their temple is finished. The members of the congregation come together to light the Ner Tamid, the eternal light, and to dedicate the new synagogue to God with a special prayer of thanks. All the congregants feel proud of their new house of worship, a temple for themselves, their children, and their children's children.

Now let us visit a House of God together.

Chapter Six

Inside God's House

Feel the quiet! Feel how the synagogue is filled with joy, love, and peace!

People have come here to welcome Shabbat. Shabbat is a holy day of peace and gladness. On Shabbat Jews worship together through prayers, songs, and blessings.

The Shabbat service is about to begin. The rabbi enters. Often a chazan (cantor) or other men and women help lead the service. The chazan and the choir sing the songs of the service. Everyone joins them and sings thanks to God. Some of the prayers and songs are in Hebrew. Others are in English.

The rabbi or chazan lifts a tall, silver cup filled with wine and sings the Kiddush. The Kiddush is a special blessing for Shabbat. It is beautiful to hear and often the congregation sings it too. Then the rabbi talks to the people and teaches them about our religion. Everyone stands and looks toward the Holy Ark. The Ark is at the center of the wall, facing the people. Inside the Holy Ark is something all Jews know is very precious, the Torah, our most important book.

Chapter Seven

The Ark Faces
the Congregation

The Holy Ark is the most important part of the synagogue because it holds the Torah. Its Hebrew name is Aron Ha-Kodesh.

The Torah inside the Aron Kodesh tells how—a long time ago—the Jewish people received the Ten Commandments. These are ten important laws. The Torah also contains the rules for building an Aron Kodesh to hold these laws.

In the days of Moses, when the Jewish people lived in the desert, the Aron Kodesh was a box covered with gold inside and out. When they moved from place to place, they carried the Aron Kodesh with poles at each corner. It always went with them. When they stopped, they put up a special tent for the Aron Kodesh. The tent, the Aron Kodesh, and the place around it were called the Tabernacle.

Today the Ark is not moved. It is no longer a box. It is more like a closet or cupboard.

Holy arks are beautiful. They may have doors of wood, marble, or gold. They may have curtains. The shelves and walls inside the Ark are covered with fine satin, velvet, or rich wood.

Milton Horn, sculptor; Estelle Horn, photographer

Chapter Eight

The Parochet Is the Curtain of the Holy Ark

Moses first put a curtain in the Tabernacle in front of the Holy Ark. He called it a parochet. Ever since, the curtain in front of the Holy Ark has been called by that Hebrew name.

The curtains for the Aron Kodesh are beautiful. Made of rich velvet, satin, or silk, they are sewn with the finest thread—silver or gold.

A parochet may be long, hanging from the ceiling to the floor, or it may be short. It usually has a design on it, sometimes a picture of a lion, a deer, or a tree, surrounded by a wide border of gold thread woven throughout the cloth. Often a Hebrew saying is sewn into the cloth.

Sometimes a parochet is handwoven and embroidered. Sometimes it is made of stained glass. But it is always beautiful. The parochet is made beautiful to honor the Torahs behind it.

Av Rivel, photographer

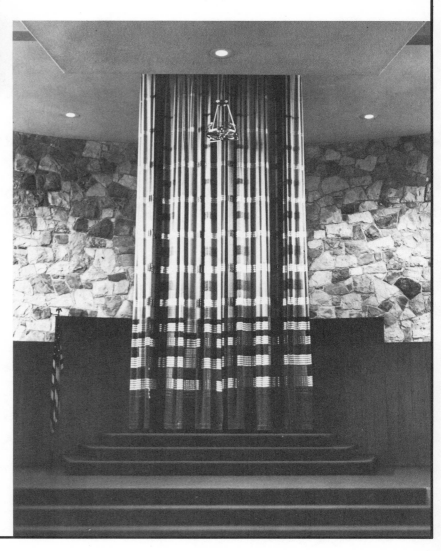

Chapter Nine

What Is the Torah?

The Torah is a big book—but it is not like any book you know. It has no pages. Instead, it is written on a long roll. That is why it is called a scroll.

The Torah is not a single book. It is five books. That is why it is so thick.

The Torah is about God and the Jewish people. It tells how the Jewish people began and how Moses led the Jews out of Egypt and taught us God's laws. That is why the Torah is also called the Five Books of Moses.

The Torah is so big that it is divided into fifty-four parts. Each part is called a sidrah. One sidrah is read every Shabbat morning in the synagogue. The Torah is read completely each year—and over again the following year, and every year. On Simchat Torah the last sidrah is read and immediately the Torah scroll is rolled back to the beginning, and the reading begins all over again! Simchat Torah is the holiday celebrating this event.

Chapter Ten

Looking Closely at a Torah Scroll

All synagogues have Torah scrolls. Every Torah scroll has exactly the same words, but sometimes they are written in bigger or smaller letters. Some Torahs are big, others are small. Every Torah scroll is written in the same language—Hebrew.

Torah scrolls used to be written on thick leather. Today, the fine skin of sheep or goats is used. It is carefully washed, scraped, dried, and split. Then it is called parchment. A Torah is too long to fit on one piece of parchment. That is why many separate pieces of parchment are used. They are sewn together to make a long scroll.

Each end of the scroll is then tied to a wooden roller. We call each of these rollers an etz chayim, a tree of life.

Sometimes the Torah is called Etz Chayim as well. This is because Jews think of the Torah as a strong tree. A tree gives us fruit, nuts, shade, and wood. People need trees to live. And we Jews need our Torah to live.

Chapter Eleven

The Sofer Writes a Torah

A long, long time ago, the Torah was not written down. Jews learned its words by heart. They taught them to their children. And the children grew up and taught their children. And then after many years, the words were written down.

Today, the Torah is written on parchment. A person who writes it is called a sofer. The sofer must not make up words. Nor must the sofer leave out words. That is why the sofer says each word aloud before writing it. The rabbis made many rules for copying the Torah. Over 800 years ago, a great rabbi, Moses Maimonides, put all the rules together in one book. Every sofer must follow these rules.

A sofer must use a special ink, made from the juices of berries and vegetables, and a special long pen, made from the feather of a turkey or goose.

A sofer may not cross out anything. If the sofer misspells the name of God, it cannot be erased. The sofer must begin all over again on a new piece of parchment. Sometimes it takes a sofer a whole year to finish one Torah scroll.

Chapter Twelve

The Mantle of the Torah

Many scrolls have special, fitted covers made of velvet or satin. These covers are called Torah mantles.

The mantle is made of rich colors—blue, red, purple, or gold. For the High Holy Days, the Torah scrolls wear white mantles. The white color stands for purity or goodness.

After the Torah scroll is read, it is rolled up. A piece of silk or linen holds the two rollers together. The mantle fits over the top of the Torah. It has two round holes at the top for the rollers to fit through.

Jews have always loved to sew pictures and designs on Torah mantles. A favorite one is a lion or, sometimes, two lions. The lion stands for the tribe of Judah, the tribe of the kings. The Torah is as important as a king—so it, too, has lions.

Other mantles have pictures of deer, flowers, the two tablets of the Ten Commandments, or the Shabbat candles with two hands spread out in blessing over them. Sometimes, sayings from the Torah are sewn on the fabric with gold or silver thread.

Chapter Thirteen

Torah Decorations— The Yad and the Breastplate

A silver chain hangs around the Torah rollers like a long necklace. The chain holds a long rod of silver, gold, or ivory that has a tiny metal or ivory hand with a pointing finger at the end. The word for "hand" in Hebrew is yad, so we call this rod a yad.

How is a yad used? It is used as a pointer. Torah readers may not use their fingers to keep their place while reading from the scroll. The oil on a fingertip may leave a mark on the parchment. Instead, readers use the tiny finger of the yad to point to each letter.

On another chain around the rollers hangs a big, flat piece of silver. This is a breastplate called a tsits. Long ago, when the Jews had the great Temple in Jerusalem, the high priest wore a breastplate like this across his chest. Today, only the Torah wears a breastplate. Often it has tiny bells hanging from it. Long ago, when the Torah was carried around, the ringing bells reminded the people to stand up in honor of the word of God within the Torah. Today, too, when the tiny bells ring, the people stand in the same way.

When a synagogue has many Torah scrolls, one may be set aside for a special holiday. Then its breastplate has the name of that holiday on it in a special holder.

Chapter Fourteen

Rimonim, Bells, and Keter

Do you hear the sound of bells? The sound may be coming from the breastplate, or it may be coming from two tall, silver headpieces which we call rimonim.

Rimonim fit over each of the two Torah rollers. Inside and outside the rimonim hang little silver bells. When the Torah is lifted, the bells ring softly. The bells say to the people: "It is time to hear the words of the Torah. Stand up! Stand up to honor the Torah."

The Torah is considered the king of all Jewish books. So, like a king, it may sometimes wear a crown. The word in Hebrew for "crown" is keter. We call this silver crown on the Torah by that Hebrew name: keter. The rimonim come in twos. There is one to fit over each Torah roller. But a Torah has only one keter. It fits over both rollers at one time.

Chapter Fifteen

The Menorah

Beautiful, tall candleholders are called menorahs. Often there are two, one on each side of the Aron Kodesh. Menorahs are not all alike. Just as we have many kinds of lamps in our homes, so we have many kinds of menorahs. Some menorahs hold little cups of oil. Other menorahs hold candles. And still others hold electric light bulbs or tubes. All have arms or branches to hold up their many lights.

Count the branches on the menorah. Does it have seven branches? Most menorahs in synagogues today have seven branches.

Why seven? Perhaps because there is a branch for each day of the week. It might be because the gold menorahs in the great Temple in Jerusalem so long ago had seven branches. Those menorahs burned olive oil. Every morning priests came to fill the oil cups.

There are some menorahs with eight branches. They are the Chanukah menorahs. They have eight branches and another branch for the shamash candle. The shamash candle is used to light the other candles on each of the eight days of Chanukah. Chanukah is the holiday honoring the freedom won by the Maccabees.

Menorahs can be made of gold, silver, copper, brass, bronze, or wood with metal cups for the lights. Their shapes are as different as the artists who create them.

Calvin Albert, artist; Oliver Baker, photographer

Chapter Sixteen

The Ner Tamid—
The Eternal Light

One light in the synagogue never goes out. It burns day and night. It is always there, glowing softly. It is never turned off. It is called a Ner Tamid—an eternal, everlasting light. Every synagogue in the world has a light like this hanging over the Holy Ark.

Moses placed a Ner Tamid in the Tabernacle, the tent where the first Ark was kept. Ever since then, a Ner Tamid has burned in the synagogue over the Ark.

Ner Tamids are of many shapes and sizes; they are made of gold, silver, brass, copper, or a mixture of metals. Some have jewels or colored glass; others are cut out to let light come through in beautiful patterns. Some use a gas flame; some, a candle; others, oil or electricity. The light is always there, shining on the Hebrew words above the Holy Ark. These words say either, "Know before whom you stand," or, "I have set God always before me."

Chapter Seventeen

The Tablets of the Law—The Ten Commandments

The Torah tells us that God gave the Jews many laws.

Of all these, the ten most important are called the Ten Commandments. Moses placed the Ten Commandments, which were written on two stone tablets, inside the Holy Ark in the Tabernacle. These tablets were called the Tablets of the Law.

Many years later, the tablets were lost. But the people remembered the Ten Commandments, and, when the Torah was written, they put them in the Torah. The Ten Commandments taught them how to live together as Jews.

To help people remember the Ten Commandments, some synagogues have arks with doors shaped like the stone tablets of Moses. Sometimes the words of the Ten Commandments are sewn into the parochet with gold or silver thread.

Because some of the laws of the Ten Commandments are too long to fit on the curtain or the Ark, only the first words or letters of each law may be contained there.

Chapter Eighteen

Art in the Synagogue— Early Times

When Moses built the Tabernacle, he called in two skillful artists. "Make the Tabernacle beautiful," he told Bezalel and Oholiab. Both men knew how to work with silver, gold, wood, and stone. They wove fine cloth in brilliant colors and built a beautiful Tabernacle.

Ever since, Jews have tried to make their temples places of beauty where they can come together to meet, to pray, and to study.

We learn about early synagogues by looking at what remains of very old ones. At a place called Dura-Europos, archaeologists dug up a synagogue built more than 1,700 years ago. The walls are covered with wonderful paintings telling stories from the Torah.

Other archaeologists, digging at Bet Alpha in the land of Israel, found a synagogue built 1,400 years ago. The floor was made of thousands of bits of colored stones, fitted together and called "mosaics." These mosaics were like painted pictures which tell many Bible stories.

Frank J. Darmstaedter, photographer

Chapter Nineteen

Art in the Synagogues Today

Today temples and synagogues bring together great artists and builders. They share their talents by creating beautiful work. No temple is quite like any other. Of course each one has an Aron Kodesh, a Ner Tamid, and a Torah, but none is exactly like any other because the artists and builders bring their own creating gift to their work.

Many of their ideas come from Jewish history. Their art reminds us that we are a very old religion. In the synagogue there are often designs of the Burning Bush, a menorah, a Ner Tamid, a Magen David, and the Lion of Judah.

And on the library and classroom walls there are often carved or painted outspread hands blessing Shabbat candles, or you can see a shofar, the curved ram's horn blown on the High Holy Days. Some metals—brass, copper, silver, and gold—may be twisted to make special decorations. If you look closely at them, you may find they have the shapes of Hebrew letters. They remind us of important Jewish values, commandments, or words of the prophets.

Some temples have museums of sacred books, megillot (scrolls), and mantles given to the temple by the first founders of the congregation. They brought those sacred objects with them when they first came to America.

Milton Horn, sculptor; Estelle Horn, photographer

Chapter Twenty

Praying from a Book

When we pray ourselves, we can make up our own prayers. But in the synagogue, when many Jews come together to pray, all of us say the same prayers at the same time. We read from a prayer book, a siddur. Siddur means "order," the order of the prayers.

Long ago, Jews did not use prayer books. The people learned the important prayers by heart.

About a thousand years ago, a great rabbi named Amram gathered all the prayers together and wrote them all down in one book.

Later when people learned to print books, these prayer books were printed. The prayers in the prayer book were not all written by one person. Some come from the Bible. Some were written by rabbis. Other prayers were poems people wanted to remember. Even when the prayers were collected and written down in a book, Jews kept writing new prayers.

Over the years, the prayer book has continued to grow and change. In every siddur, there are many important prayers printed in Hebrew. For many Jews, Hebrew is the most important language of prayer.

Chapter Twenty-one

What's inside a Siddur?

The siddur has many different prayers for many different occasions and purposes.

Some prayers praise God's goodness and mercy: "Praise the Lord, to whom all praise is due." Some prayers give thanks for all that God has given us—the Torah, wine, bread. They begin: "Blessed are You, O Lord our God."

Other prayers ask God for help and protection: "Grant us peace, Your most precious gift."

Special prayers comfort us in times of sorrow. They remind us that God is always near: "The Lord is my Shepherd, I shall not want."

There are prayers to tell us what to do or remember: "You shall love the Lord, your God, with all your heart, with all your soul, and with all your might."

Most prayers of the siddur say "us" and "our," not "me" or "I," because all Jews are one people and we pray together in the synagogue. Even when we pray alone, we should never forget to care about all our fellow Jews everywhere.

Chapter Twenty-two

The Shema

A long time ago, people prayed to many gods—to the sun or the moon, to trees or rocks, or to statues.

Then the Jewish people sought and found only One God—the One God to whom we pray.

Moses taught the Jewish people that there is only one God. And the words he used are in the Torah. Every Jew knows these words and says them throughout life. Those words form the prayer we call the Shema:

"Hear, O Israel: the Lord is our God, the Lord is One!"

"Shema Yisrael, Adonai Elohenu, Adonai Echad!"

YOUR GOODNESS AND LOVE

אהבת עולם

אַהֲבַת עוֹלָם בֵּית יִשְׂרָאֵל עַמְּךָ אָהָבְתָּ: תּוֹרָה וּמִצְוֹת, חֻקִּים
וּמִשְׁפָּטִים אוֹתָנוּ לִמַּדְתָּ.
עַל־כֵּן, יְיָ אֱלֹהֵינוּ, בְּשָׁכְבֵּנוּ וּבְקוּמֵנוּ נָשִׂיחַ בְּחֻקֶּיךָ, וְנִשְׂמַח
בְּדִבְרֵי תוֹרָתֶךָ וּבְמִצְוֹתֶיךָ לְעוֹלָם וָעֶד.
כִּי הֵם חַיֵּינוּ וְאֹרֶךְ יָמֵינוּ, וּבָהֶם נֶהְגֶּה יוֹמָם וָלָיְלָה, וְאַהֲבָתְךָ
אַל־תָּסִיר מִמֶּנּוּ לְעוֹלָמִים: בָּרוּךְ אַתָּה, יְיָ, אוֹהֵב עַמּוֹ יִשְׂרָאֵל.

You are our God, the Source of life and its blessings. Wherever we turn our gaze, we behold signs of Your goodness and love.

The whole universe proclaims Your glory. Your loving spirit hovers over all Your works, guiding and sustaining them.

The harmony and grandeur of nature speak to us of You; the beauty and truth of Torah reveal Your will to us. You are the One and Eternal God of time and space!

• •

שְׁמַע יִשְׂרָאֵל: יְיָ אֱלֹהֵינוּ, יְיָ אֶחָד!

Hear, O Israel: the Lord is our God, the Lord is One!

בָּרוּךְ שֵׁם כְּבוֹד מַלְכוּתוֹ לְעוֹלָם וָעֶד!

Blessed is His glorious kingdom for ever and ever!

All are seated

וְאָהַבְתָּ אֵת יְיָ אֱלֹהֶיךָ בְּכָל־לְבָבְךָ וּבְכָל־נַפְשְׁךָ וּבְכָל־מְאֹדֶךָ.
וְהָיוּ הַדְּבָרִים הָאֵלֶּה, אֲשֶׁר אָנֹכִי מְצַוְּךָ הַיּוֹם, עַל־לְבָבֶךָ.
וְשִׁנַּנְתָּם לְבָנֶיךָ, וְדִבַּרְתָּ בָּם בְּשִׁבְתְּךָ בְּבֵיתֶךָ, וּבְלֶכְתְּךָ
בַדֶּרֶךְ, וּבְשָׁכְבְּךָ וּבְקוּמֶךָ.

You shall love the Lord your God with all your mind, with all your strength, with all your being.

194

Set these words, which I command you this day, upon your heart. Teach them faithfully to your children; speak of them in your home and on your way, when you lie down and when you rise up.

וּקְשַׁרְתָּם לְאוֹת עַל־יָדֶךָ, וְהָיוּ לְטֹטָפֹת בֵּין עֵינֶיךָ, וּכְתַבְתָּם
עַל־מְזֻזוֹת בֵּיתֶךָ, וּבִשְׁעָרֶיךָ.

Bind them as a sign upon your hand; let them be a symbol before your eyes; inscribe them on the doorposts of your house, and on your gates.

לְמַעַן תִּזְכְּרוּ וַעֲשִׂיתֶם אֶת־כָּל־מִצְוֹתָי, וִהְיִיתֶם קְדֹשִׁים
לֵאלֹהֵיכֶם. אֲנִי יְיָ אֱלֹהֵיכֶם, אֲשֶׁר הוֹצֵאתִי אֶתְכֶם מֵאֶרֶץ
מִצְרַיִם לִהְיוֹת לָכֶם לֵאלֹהִים. אֲנִי יְיָ אֱלֹהֵיכֶם.

Be mindful of all My Mitzvot, and do them: so shall you consecrate yourselves to your God. I, the Lord, am your God who led you out of Egypt to be your God; I, the Lord, am your God.

• •

FREE TO SING

גאולה

אֱמֶת וֶאֱמוּנָה כָּל־זֹאת, וְקַיָּם עָלֵינוּ כִּי הוּא יְיָ אֱלֹהֵינוּ וְאֵין
זוּלָתוֹ, וַאֲנַחְנוּ יִשְׂרָאֵל עַמּוֹ.

*Eternal truth it is that You alone are God,
and there is none else.*

*May the righteous of all nations rejoice in Your love
and exult in Your justice.*

הַפּוֹדֵנוּ מִיַּד מְלָכִים, מַלְכֵּנוּ הַגּוֹאֲלֵנוּ מִכַּף כָּל־הֶעָרִיצִים.
הָעֹשֶׂה גְדֹלוֹת עַד אֵין חֵקֶר, וְנִפְלָאוֹת עַד אֵין מִסְפָּר.

*Let them beat their swords into plowshares;
Let them beat their spears into pruninghooks.*

195

Chapter Twenty-three

Singing Songs to God

Singing is another way of praying to God.

Jews were often joyful when they thought about God. They made up many songs of praise. One said, "Who is like You, God?" We Jews still sing this very old song—Mi Chamochah.

The songs Jews sing to God are not always happy. Some have sad melodies, like the Kol Nidre on Yom Kippur eve. Other songs are proud ones, like the Adon Olam. This means, "Lord of the universe." One of the best known is En Kelohenu, "There is none like our God."

The songs of praise are called hymns. They began as poems set to music a long time ago. Today composers take these beautiful old melodies and weave them into new songs. New music is written and new musical services are created by young talents. They become part of synagogue music.

The person who leads the singing in the synagogue is the chazan, the cantor. The chazan may sing alone or with a choir or with the entire congregation.

One kind of singing heard in the synagogue is different from all other singing. It has music like a song, but it has no clear beginning or end. The notes go up and down. It grows louder, then softer, and it is often repeated. This is called chanting. Chants are the oldest Jewish music. The rhythm of chanting often makes the congregation sway forward and back.

Chapter Twenty-four

Playing Songs to God

David, a shepherd boy, prayed by creating songs to God. Later, when David became king over Israel, he had a son, Solomon. Like his father, Solomon became king and remembered the songs (called psalms) of his father, David. When Solomon built the great Temple in Jerusalem, Jews came to pray and to worship God. And in the Temple they sang the psalms of David. Sometimes they played the harp, the lute, the lyre, the cymbals, and the drums.

More than 2,000 years ago, the great Temple was destroyed. For a long time the Jews were so sad that they wanted no musical instruments in their services. They sang songs to God, but without instruments. The years went by and the Jews in America felt that the joy of music belonged in their services again. That is why, in many temples today, there is an organ, violin, flute, or other instrument which reminds us of the human voice and of David's songs. And on special holidays, one can sometimes hear the sound of a harp, a trumpet, or many violins blending with the choir.

Every temple has one instrument which makes a loud, solemn blast. It is the shofar, the ram's horn.

In ancient times, in the desert, the shofar was used to call the people together. Today, the shofar is blown on the High Holy Days. It is a call to prayer. It also reminds us to try to live a better life.

Chapter Twenty-five

Why Do We Go to the Synagogue?

Jews go to the synagogue for many reasons:
> to pray,
>> to study,
>>> to meet.

To pray—at any time. Shabbat is a day of prayer for all Jews. Other times we are drawn to the synagogue for celebrations with other families and to share the ceremonies of our own lives. We may come to pray to God when we have troubles or are grateful.

To study—to understand how Jews came to be, to learn our prayers, our history, our festivals, and what it means to be a Jew in today's world. We begin as children, but we keep on studying for a lifetime. Jews need and want to learn as well as to share what they have learned with each other.

To meet—our community, our friends, our neighbors, and our relatives. In praying, working, and learning together, we meet younger and older people. We attend classes and meetings of the temple Brotherhood, Youth Group, Sisterhood, Senior Citizens Group, and Child and Day Care Center groups as well as many other groups of people. We need each other, and we help each other in quiet and wonderful ways. In synagogues people learn how to care for one another. There they feel at home.

The temple is a special place of learning, giving, and growing.

Chapter Twenty-six

The Family

Many families have a father and a mother, a son or a daughter. Other families have only one parent. In some, grandparents and other relatives share the home. All of them come together to celebrate ceremonies and holidays. Some celebrations take place in the home. Many more are shared with members of the congregation at the synagogue.

Shabbat is celebrated both at home and in the synagogue. Each member of the family has a part and each person enjoys the gift of Shabbat—its peace, its renewal, and its prayers. We light the Shabbat candles to greet Shabbat at sundown on Friday evening. We raise the wine cup for the blessing over the wine; we recite or chant a blessing over the chalah, the twisted loaf of Shabbat bread, and we share it. Then we share the Shabbat meal.

At the synagogue, the week's Torah portion is read aloud. Shabbat afternoon brings music, study, learning, both at home and in the synagogue. At sundown during the Havdalah service, we smell spices, taste sweet wine, and light the Havdalah candle bringing our family's home celebration of Shabbat to a close. We honor the Shabbat to keep it holy.

Chapter Twenty-seven

The Rabbi Is a Teacher

The word rabbi is Hebrew for "my teacher."

Rabbis are teachers...who tell and show us what it means to be a Jew.

    ...who talk to the very young and the very old.

    ...who share what they know about our Jewish religion and history.

    ...who study and can explain the meaning of Torah, so we know how to live by Torah's laws today.

    ...who were taught in a special school and continue to study for a lifetime.

Rabbis are friends...who listen and help us.

    ...who are not afraid to tell the truth about what is wrong and what is right.

Rabbis are leaders...who are part of each Jewish person's life. During the most important times of our lives, the rabbi's prayers lead us. We take with us the prayers we heard at Bar or Bat Mitzvah, Confirmation, and at our wedding.

    ...who teach the Jews the way to serve God.

    ...who work with others to help make life better in the community.

All these years the Jewish people have turned to their teachers, the rabbis. After the Temple was gone, it was the rabbis who taught the people and held them together. Then, as now, it is the rabbis who call out for courage to live as Jews.

Follow the dots.
What do you see?
Color the picture.

The braided loaf is called a *ḥallah.*
We say the blessing over bread together:
Baruch Ata Adonai Ehlohay-nu Melech Ha-olam Hamotzi
Leḥem Meen Ha-aretz.
Praised be Thou, O Lord our God, who bringest forth
bread from the earth.

Father sings the *Kiddush*.
The *Kiddush* is a blessing over wine.
The Sabbath is sweet and good like wine.
After singing the *Kiddush*, Father blesses the children.

Co-published by Behrman House, Inc. & Winston Press, Inc.

Our Synagogue

THE SABBATH

It is Friday night.
The sun is going down.
Our Sabbath begins.
It will last until Saturday evening.
Mother lights the candles.

Chapter Twenty-eight

The Celebration of Ceremonies in the Synagogue

There are celebrations and ceremonies which we share within the synagogue. The ceremonies mark special days in our lives with music, prayers, and tradition. They celebrate the gift of life and its changes, joy and sadness.

When we are born, there is often a Berit Milah or a Berit Ha-Chayim. When babies are named, the rabbi says a prayer and a blessing for them.

When we start religious school, we are consecrated in a ceremony which begins our understanding of how Jews live and study in the synagogue. We become part of the world of Jewish learning.

When we celebrate our Bar or Bat Mitzvah, when we reach the age of thirteen we become full members of the congregation.

At our Confirmation service, celebrated on the anniversary of the day Moses received the Ten Commandments on Mt. Sinai, we promise to live as Jews, to study, and to follow the laws of Torah.

Chapter Twenty-nine

What Is
a Synagogue?

Synagogues are the places where Jews come together to meet, to study, and to pray to God. Some may be small; others, large. Some may be very simple; others may have rich designs and rise up, with a rounded dome, towards the sky. Some may have all pillars or flat roofs. Some are made of brick or wood. Some may be quite different. But, inside, the things that have meaning to those who come are always there.

These things are:
A Torah, an Ark, a Ner Tamid, a menorah, the Tablets of the Law, a school, and a feeling of holiness.

It does not really matter if a synagogue is large or small, simple or ornate. What matters is that the Jews who go there love God and the Jewish people with all their heart. We learn about our tradition and what it means to us and to our families. We learn how to do good deeds and to care about others.

> We learn about God.
> We pray to God.
> We learn what it means to be a Jew.

Hebrew Words

Hebrew Word	English Pronunciation and Meaning	Chapter
אֲדוֹן עוֹלָם	**ADON OLAM.** An old song sung in the synagogue. The words mean "Lord of the universe."	23
אֲרוֹן הַקֹּדֶשׁ	**ARON HA-KODESH.** The place in the temple where Jews keep the Holy Torah. The words mean "the Holy Ark."	7, 19
בַּר/בַּת מִצְוָה	**BAR/BAT MITZVAH.** The ceremony at which a thirteen-year-old becomes a full member of the congregation, obligated to perform the commandments.	5, 27, 28
בִּימָה	**BIMAH.** The raised platform in a synagogue where Jews stand to read the Torah. In some old synagogues, the **bimah** is in the very center. In others, the **bimah** is in the front, like a stage.	4
חַזָּן	**CHAZAN.** The cantor.	6, 23
אֵין כֵּאלֹהֵינוּ	**EN KELOHENU.** An old song sung in the synagogue. The words mean "there is none like our God."	23
עֵץ חַיִּים	**ETZ CHAYIM.** The wooden rollers of the Torah scroll. The words mean "tree of life." Sometimes we call the Torah itself "**Etz Chayim.**"	10
הַבְדָּלָה	**HAVDALAH.** The service concluding Shabbat at which we say the **Havdalah** prayer over a cup of wine, smell spices, and light a **Havdalah** candle.	26
כֶּתֶר	**KETER.** A crown. A king wears a **keter,** and so does the Torah.	14
קִדּוּשׁ	**KIDDUSH.** The special blessing over the wine on Shabbat and holidays.	6
כָּל נִדְרֵי	**KOL NIDRE.** The prayer sung in the synagogue on Yom Kippur eve. The words mean "all promises."	23
מְנוֹרָה	**MENORAH.** The lamp in the synagogue for holding candles, light bulbs, or little cups of oil. Most have seven branches, but the **menorah** for Chanukah has eight branches plus a place for the shamash candle.	15
מִי כָמֹכָה	**MI CHAMOCHAH.** A song of praise to God which comes from the Bible. The words mean "who is like You, God?"	23

Hebrew Word	English Pronunciation and Meaning	Chapter
מָגֵן דָּוִד	**MAGEN DAVID.** A star with six points. The words mean "shield of David."	19
נֵר תָּמִיד	**NER TAMID.** The light that always burns in the synagogue. The words mean "the light that is always lit."	16, 19
פָּרֹכֶת	**PAROCHET.** The curtain which hangs in front of the Holy Ark.	8
רִמּוֹנִים	**RIMONIM.** The two tall, silver headpieces with bells that fit over the two Torah rollers. The word means "pomegranates" because they used to be shaped round, like that fruit.	14
שַׁבָּת	**SHABBAT.** The Sabbath, a holy day of peace and gladness.	6, 19, 26
שַׁמָּשׁ	**SHAMASH.** The word means "servant." So, one who serves the synagogue to make sure things go right is called a **shamash.** The extra candle in the Chanukah menorah is called a **shamash** because it serves to light the other candles.	15
שְׁמַע	**SHEMA.** The most important prayer in the Torah. It gets its name from the first word of the prayer, **Shema,** which means "Hear!"	22
סִדּוּר	**SIDDUR.** The prayer book. The word means "order." The prayer book gives us all the prayers in the right order.	20, 21
סִדְרָה	**SIDRAH.** The part of the Torah we read each Shabbat. The Torah is divided into fifty-four **sidrot.**	9
שׁוֹפָר	**SHOFAR.** The curved ram's horn which is blown in the synagogue on the High Holy Days.	24
סוֹפֵר	**SOFER.** The person who copies the words of the Torah and writes them on a Torah scroll. The word means "writer."	11
תּוֹרָה	**TORAH.** The first five books of the Bible. Sometimes we call them the "Five Books of Moses." They make up the **Torah,** the most important Jewish book.	9, 10, 11, 12, 13, 14
צִיץ	**TSITS.** A flat piece of silver or gold which decorates the front of the Torah. The word means "breastplate."	13
יָד	**YAD.** The little pointer used when reading the Torah. The word means "hand." The end of the **yad** often looks like a tiny hand with one finger pointing.	13